# ACCA

## Paper P2 (INT & UK)

### Corporate Reporting

Pocket Notes

## British library cataloguing-in-publication data

A catalogue record for this book is available from the British Library.

Published by:
Kaplan Publishing UK
Unit 2 The Business Centre
Molly Millars Lane
Wokingham
Berkshire
RG41 2QZ

ISBN 978-1-78415-854-5

© Kaplan Financial Limited, 2017

Printed and bound in Great Britain.

# Contents

This document references IFRS® Standards and IAS® Standards, which are authored by the International Accounting Standards Board (the Board), and published in the 2016 IFRS Standards Red Book.

## The exam

This exam will test your knowledge of accounting concepts, principles and theories. You will be expected to comment on scenarios and assess proposed accounting treatments.

You must be able to apply accounting theory to practical situations and will be expected to cover several accounting standards in one scenario. You must study the breadth of the syllabus.

A knowledge of current issues is required.

The exam is three hours and 15 minutes.

**Section A (50%)** – one case study compulsory question (50 marks).

- This will be a scenario based question dealing with the preparation of consolidated financial statements including group cash flow statements and financial reporting issues.

**Section B (50%)** – A choice of two question from a total of three (25 marks each).

- In this section, two questions will be scenario or case study based and one question will be essay based. They will cover all aspects of the syllabus.

- You must ensure you revise the breadth of the syllabus, as questions are likely to cover more than one topic.

- Two professional marks will be available in each of the Section B questions of the exam. They will be awarded for clarity and quality of discussion.

# Keys to Success in Paper P2

## Exercising judgement / technique

- On the compulsory question, make sure you have a thorough knowledge of all aspects of group accounting. Use your groups technique to work through the question methodically, focusing on the parts you can do. Don't panic if there are adjustments that you do not know what to do with, better to leave them and get on with the rest of the question, rather than get bogged down. Don't spend too long on the consolidation as you still have to complete the rest of the question.

- Keep up to date with current issues. You may have a question that covers a single new standard or exposure draft.

- Try and step back from question scenarios and think of all of the possible impacts. It is unlikely the Examiner will give you a scenario where only one accounting standard should be applied. It is more likely to be two or three so you must recognise this and produce a valid argument for your proposed accounting treatment.

## Exam focus

- Read around the subject, (Student Accountant, ACCA website, accountancy journals).

- Practice exam questions.

- Spend an equal amount of time on each question in the exam

- There will be things in the exam you have never seen before. If you don't know what to do, don't waste time on them.

## UK syllabus students

The majority of the UK syllabus paper will be the same as the international paper, which is based on International Financial Reporting Standards. There will also be some key differences between UK standards and the IFRS for SMEs standard examined in the UK paper, as well as some Companies Act requirements, but it is anticipated that the differences will account for no more than 20% in Paper P2.

UK syllabus students should refer to the list of examinable documents for the UK examination available on the ACCA web site at www.accaglobal.com.

To assist UK syllabus students, this publication includes UK GAAP content in chapter 25.

Quality and accuracy are of the utmost importance to us so if you spot an error in any of our products, please send an email to mykaplanreporting@kaplan.com with full details, or follow the link to the feedback form in MyKaplan.

Our Quality Co-ordinator will work with our technical team to verify the error and take action to ensure it is corrected in future editions.

## Frameworks

In this chapter

- Overview.
- Conceptual Framework for Financial Reporting 2010.
- IFRS 13 Fair Value Measurement.

## Overview

- This chapter gives useful information relating to the Conceptual Framework for Financial Reporting, which includes definitions of the elements of financial statements.

- The chapter also provides information on IFRS 13 Fair Value Measurement

## Conceptual Framework for Financial Reporting 2010

The **Conceptual Framework for Financial Reporting** identifies the principles on which accounting standards are to be developed. It aims to assist in the preparation of financial statements, development of new standards and to reduce alternative accounting treatments.

- The financial statements are normally prepared on the assumption that an entity is a going concern and will continue in operation for the foreseeable future.

Qualitative characteristics of useful financial information

Fundamental characteristics:
- Relevance
- Faithful representation

Enhancing characteristics:
- Verifiability
- Timeliness
- Understandability
- Comparability

Elements relating to financial position

**Assets**
Resources controlled by an entity from a past event that will lead to a probable inflow of economic benefits.

**Liabilities**
Present obligations of an entity from a past event that will lead to a probable outflow of economic benefits.

**Equity**
The residual interest in an entity's net assets.

Elements relating to financial performance

**Incomes**
Increases in economic benefits during an accounting period.

**Expenses**
Decreases in economic benefits during an accounting period.

**Recognition** of an item in the financial statements occurs if:

- the item meets the definition of an element of financial statements
- it is probable that any future economic benefit associated with the item will flow to or from the entity
- it can be measured at a monetary amount with sufficient reliability.

### Current issue – Exposure draft on the Conceptual Framework

Among the topics covered are:

- Revised definitions of assets and liabilities
- Guidance on derecognition of the elements
- Principles for distinguishing profit or loss from other comprehensive income.

### Exam focus

You will find the Framework useful in the exam. Use it to determine whether the exam scenario results in elements which meet the definitions and which, therefore, should be recognised.

## IFRS 13 Fair Value Measurement

**Definition**

Fair value is defined as '**the price that would be received to sell an asset or paid to transfer a liability in an orderly transaction between market participants at the measurement date**' (IFRS 13, para 9).

### Fair value hierarchy

**Level 1 inputs**
- Quoted prices for identical assets in active markets

**Level 2 inputs**
- Quoted prices for identical assets in less active markets
- Quoted prices for similar assets in active markets

**Level 3 inputs**
- Unobservable inputs

Priority is given to level 1 inputs when determining fair value.

## Markets

IFRS 13 says that fair value should be determined by reference to the principal market.

This is the market with the greatest volume of activity.

If the principal market cannot be determined then fair value should be measured based on the price in the most advantageous market.

## Non-financial assets

Non-financial assets include:

- Property, plant and equipment
- Intangible assets

The fair value of a non-financial asset should be based on its **highest and best use.**

Exam focus

Recent examination questions on fair values include

- March / June 2016 – Mehran
- June 2015 – Yanong

# 2

## The professional and ethical duty of the accountant

**In this chapter**

- Overview.
- Ethical issues facing the accountant.
- Ethical codes of conduct.
- Consequences of unethical behaviour.

## Overview

- **Ethics** are an important part of working as an accountant.
- Ethics is likely to come up as part of the compulsory question.
- You may be asked to comment on a particular situation and whether the directors have acted in an ethical manner.

## Ethical issues facing the accountant

Definition

Professional ethics are the principles and standards that underlie the responsibilities and conduct of a person in performing his/her function in a particular field of expertise.

- Ethical principles are important in a business organisation as they set the tone for the culture and behaviour of employees and management.
- The application of ethics can sometimes be intangible. Ethics is often described as 'doing the right thing' but this can mean different things to different individuals.

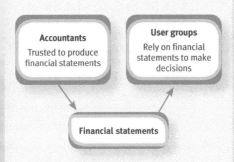

## Ethical codes of conduct

Professional accountants are bound by their Institute or Association's codes of ethics and are expected to act in accordance with such codes of conduct.

### ACCA Code of Ethics

The ACCA Code of Ethics and Conduct applies to all students, associates and members. The Code is in the form of a framework and adopts a principles-based approach; whilst some specific rules are included, compliance is largely concerned with the observation of the fundamental principles.

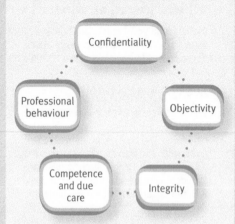

- **Professional competence and due care** – Members have a continuing duty to maintain professional knowledge and skill at a level required to ensure that a client or employer receives a competent and professional service.

- **Confidentiality** – Members should respect the confidentiality of information acquired as a result of professional and business relationships and should not disclose any such information to third parties without proper and specific authority.

- **Professional behaviour** – Members should comply with relevant laws and regulations and avoid any action that discredits the profession.

- **Integrity** – Members should be straightforward and honest in all professional and business relationships.

- **Objectivity** – Members should not allow bias, conflicts of interest or undue influence of others to override their judgement.

## Consequences of unethical behaviour

Loss of professional reputation

Disciplinary action by professional body, including expulsion

Conviction of criminal offence

CDDA Disqualification order

Court order to pay financial compensation

Exam focus

Recent exam questions include:

- March/June 2016 – Weston
- September/December 2015 – Bubble
- June 2015 – Kutchen

# 3

# Performance reporting and performance appraisal

## In this chapter

- Overview.
- IAS 1 Presentation of financial statements.
- Accounting concepts to apply in preparation of financial statements.
- IAS 8 Accounting policies, changes in accounting estimates and errors.
- IFRS 5 Non current assets held for sale and discontinued operations.
- IAS 33 Earnings per share.
- IAS 34 Interim Financial Reporting.

## Overview

- Many of these accounting standards were covered in your previous studies.

- The level of application required in this exam will be much higher.

## IAS 1 Presentation of financial statements

IAS 1 provides standard formats for the statement of profit or loss and other comprehensive income, statement of financial position and statement of changes in equity.

Note that items included within other comprehensive income for the year must be classified between:

(a) those items which may be reclassified to profit and loss in future accounting periods, and

(b) those items which will not be reclassified to profit and loss in future accounting periods.

## Accounting concepts to apply in preparation of financial statements

Going concern

Comparability

Accruals

Offsetting

Consistency

Materiality and aggregation

## IAS 8 Accounting policies, changes in accounting estimates and errors

### Selecting accounting policies

Accounting policies must be determined by applying the relevant IFRS Standard. If there is no standard, then management should choose an accounting policy that results in relevant and reliable financial information.

### Changing accounting policies

Accounting policies can only change if:

- the change is required by a standard or interpretation; or

- the change results in more relevant and reliable information.

Changes in accounting policies are accounted for retrospectively as if the new policy had always been applied.

Do not confuse a change in accounting policy with a change in estimate, such as depreciation.

### Errors

Prior period errors are misstatements due to mistakes in applying accounting policies and fraud. They are corrected retrospectively.

# IFRS 5 Non current assets held for sale and discontinued operations

 Definition

Per IFRS 5, a discontinued operation is a component of an entity that has been sold, or which is classified as held for sale, and which is

- a separate line of business, or
- part of a plan to dispose of a separate line of business, or
- a subsidiary acquired solely for resale.

### Presentation

A **single amount** for discontinued operations is presented on the face of the statement of profit or loss. This comprises:

- the post-tax profit or loss of the operation
- any profit or loss on disposal, or any loss on classification as held for sale.

# IAS 33 Earnings per share

**Basic earnings per share**

Exam focus

- You are unlikely to get a question which requires only the calculation of EPS.

**Key Point**

- Earnings per share is an important ratio that is used as a comparison for company performance and forms part of the Price / Earnings ratio.

- IAS 33 applies to all listed companies. Private companies must follow the standard if they disclose an EPS figure.

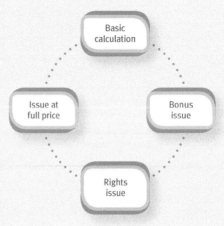

**Basic earnings per share** is calculated as:

$$\frac{\text{profit or loss for the period attributable to the equity shareholders}}{\text{weighted average number of equity shares outstanding in the period}}$$

The weighted average number of equity shares takes into account when the shares were issued in the year.

**Diluted earnings per share**

- IAS 33 requires diluted earnings per share to be disclosed as well as basic EPS.

- Diluted EPS shows the effect on the current EPS if the maximum number of potential equity shares are issued.

- Potential equity shares consist of:

  - convertible loan stock

  - share warrants and options

# IAS 34 Interim Financial Reporting

## Definition

An interim period 'is a financial reporting period that is shorter than a full financial year' (IAS 34, para 4).

IAS 34 outlines the minimum content that should be included in an interim financial report.

The minimum content to be included is:

- A condensed statement of financial position

- A condensed statement of profit or loss and other comprehensive income

- A condensed statement of changes in equity

- A condensed statement of cash flows

- Selected disclosure notes.

## Exam Focus

Recent examination questions include:

- September/December 2015 – Chemclean

- June 2015 – IAS 1 and Integrated Reporting

# Revenue

**In this chapter**

- Overview.
- IFRS 15 Revenue from contracts with customers.

## Overview

Exam focus

- Revenue recognition is a common P2 exam topic. It can appear in Section A or B of the exam.

- It is vital that you understand the revenue recognition rules and can apply them to real life scenarios.

## IFRS 15 Revenue from contracts with customers

IFRS 15 adopts a five step approach to revenue recognition:

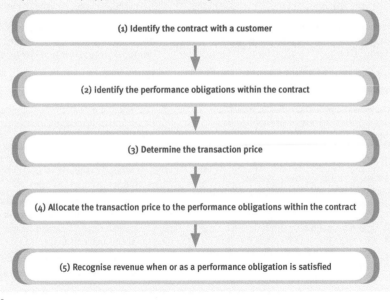

(1) Identify the contract with a customer

(2) Identify the performance obligations within the contract

(3) Determine the transaction price

(4) Allocate the transaction price to the performance obligations within the contract

(5) Recognise revenue when or as a performance obligation is satisfied

Further detail about each of these steps is provided below:

### (1) Identify the contract

A contract is an agreement between two or more parties that creates rights and obligations.

### (2) Identify the separate performance obligations within a contract

Performance obligations are promises to transfer distinct goods or services to a customer.

### (3) Determine the transaction price

The transaction price is the amount of consideration to which an entity expects to be entitled.

If this includes a variable amount it is included in the transaction price if 'it is highly probable that a significant reversal in the amount of revenue recognised will not occur when the uncertainty is resolved' (IFRS 15, para 57).

### (4) Allocate the transaction price to the performance obligations in the contract

The total transaction price should be allocated to each performance obligation in proportion to stand-alone selling prices.

### (5) Recognise revenue when (or as) a performance obligation is satisfied.

The entity must determine whether it satisfies its performance obligation over time or at a point in time.

An entity satisfies a performance obligation and recognises revenue over time, if one of the following criteria is met:

- 'the customer simultaneously receives and consumes the benefits provided by the entity's performance as the entity performs'

- 'the entity's performance creates or enhances an asset (for example, work in progress) that the customer controls as the asset is created or enhanced'

- 'the entity's performance does not create an asset with an alternative use to the entity and the entity has an enforceable right to payment for performance completed to date' (IFRS 15, para 35).

If a performance obligation is not satisfied over time then it is satisfied at the point in time when the customer obtains control of the asset. IFRS 15 says that the following are indicators of the transfer of control:

- The entity has a right to payment
- The customer has legal title
- The entity has transferred physical possession
- The customer has the significant risks and rewards of ownership
- The customer has accepted the asset.

Exam focus

Recent examination questions include:

- September/December 2015 – Revenue from contracts with customers
- June 2014 – Minco

# 5

# Non-current assets, agriculture and inventories

In this chapter

- Overview.
- IAS 16 Property, plant and equipment.
- IAS 20 Accounting for government grants and disclosure of government assistance.
- IAS 23 Borrowing costs.
- IAS 40 Investment property.
- IAS 38 Intangible assets.
- IAS 36 Impairment of assets.
- IFRS 5 Assets held for sale.
- IAS 41 Agriculture.
- IAS 2 Inventories.

## Overview

Exam focus

- This chapter focuses on standards relating to tangible and intangible assets.

- All of these have been studied previously but are regularly examined.

- This chapter is a reminder of the key points.

## IAS 16 Property, plant and equipment

Key Point

- Property, plant and equipment is initially recognised at cost.

- Subsequent expenditure on non-current assets may be capitalised if it:

  - enhances the economic benefits of the asset, e.g. adding a new wing to a building

  - replaces part of an asset that has been separately depreciated, and has been fully depreciated e.g. a furnace that requires new linings

  - replaces economic benefits previously consumed, e.g. a major inspection of aircraft.

- The asset is depreciated over its useful economic life.

  - The **depreciation method** and **useful life** of an asset should be reviewed at the end of each year.

  - If an asset has parts with **different lives**, (e.g. a building with a flat roof), the component parts of the asset should be depreciated separately.

**Revaluation of property, plant and equipment**

- Revaluation is **optional**. If one asset is revalued, all assets in that class must be revalued.

- Revaluation **gains** are credited to other comprehensive income unless the gain reverses a previous revaluation loss of the same asset previously recognised in profit or loss.

- Revaluation **losses** are charged to the statement of profit or loss unless the loss relates to a previous revaluation surplus, in which case it should be charged to other comprehensive income.

- An entity may choose to make a **reserves transfer** for the **excess depreciation** arising from a revaluation. This is taken from the revaluation reserve to retained earnings.

## IAS 20 Accounting for government grants and disclosure of government assistance

Key Point

Grants should not be recognised until there is reasonable assurance that the grant will be received and that conditions will be complied with.

- Income grants given to subsidise expenditure should be matched to the related costs.

- Grants for purchases of non-current assets should be recognised over the expected useful lives of the related assets. There are two acceptable accounting policies for this:

- deduct the grant from the cost of the asset and depreciate the net cost; o

- treat the grant as deferred income and release to the statement of prof or loss over the life of the asset.

# IAS 23 Borrowing costs

Definition

**Borrowing costs** are interest and other costs incurred when borrowing funds.

Entities **must capitalise** borrowing costs that are directly attributable to the acquisition, construction or production of assets that take a substantial amount of time to get ready for use.

# IAS 40 Investment property

Definition

**Investment property** is property held to earn rentals or for capital appreciation or both.

Investment property is initially recognised at cost.

An entity can then choose either the **cost model** (cost less depreciation) or the **fair value model**.

- The **fair value model** recognises investment properties in the statement of financial position at **fair value**. **Gains** and **losses** on revaluation are recognised in the **statement of profit or loss**.

## IAS 38 Intangible assets

Definition

An **intangible asset 'is an identifiable non-monetary asset without physical substance'** (IAS 38, para 8).

- An intangible asset is initially recognised at cost if:

  (1) It is identifiable.

  (2) It is controlled by the entity.

  (3) It will generate probable future economic benefits for the entity.

  (4) The cost can be measured reliably.

- If an intangible does not meet the recognition criteria, then it should be charged to the statement of profit or loss as expenditure is incurred.

- Intangible assets should be amortised over their useful lives.

- If it can be demonstrated that the useful life is indefinite then no amortisation should be charged but an annual impairment review must be carried out.

- Intangible assets can be revalued but only if fair values can be determined with reference to an active market.

- Costs incurred during the research must be expensed as they are incurred. Costs incurred during development should be recognised as an asset if they meet the following criteria:

  (a) the project is technically feasible

  (b) the asset will be completed then used or sold

  (c) the entity is able to use or sell the asset

(d) the asset will generate future economic benefits

(e) the entity has adequate technical, financial and other resources to complete the project

(f) the expenditure on the project can be reliably measured.

- Amortisation over the useful life of the new product or process will commence once the project is complete.

## IAS 36 Impairment of assets

### Definition

An **impairment loss** is the amount by which the carrying amount of an asset or cash-generating unit exceeds its recoverable amount.

- Impairment is measured by comparing the carrying amount of an asset with its recoverable amount.

### Key Point

- If the carrying amount exceeds the recoverable amount, the asset is impaired and must be written down.

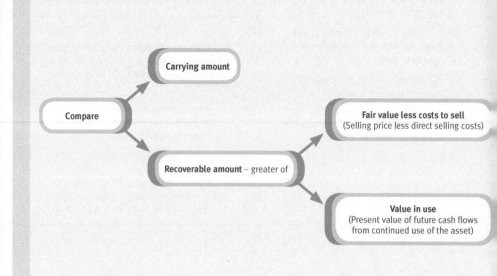

## Indicators of impairment

Impairment reviews are required where there is an indicator of impairment.

Internal Indicators:

- Physical damage to the asset.

- Management committed to reorganisation of the business.

- Idle or obsolete assets.

- Operating losses in the business where the assets are used.

External Indicators:

- Competitor actions.

- Increasing interest rates (because this reduces the value in use).

- Market values of assets falling.

## Cash-generating units (CGU)

**Key Point**

Individual assets may not generate a distinguishable cash flow. In this case the impairment calculation should be based on a CGU.

**Definition**

A **cash-generating unit** is the smallest group of assets that generates independent cash inflows.

Impairment losses on a CGU are allocated in the following order:

(1) goodwill

(2) remaining assets in proportion to carrying amounts.

No asset can be written down below the higher of fair value less costs to sell, value in use and zero.

### Recognition of impairment losses

Assets held at cost: The amount of the impairment is charged to the statement of profit or loss.

Revalued assets: The impairment is charged to other comprehensive income to reverse any previous surplus on that asset with any excess charged to profit or loss.

## IFRS 5 Assets held for sale

**Definition**

An asset should be classified as held for sale if its carrying amount will be recovered principally through a sales transaction.

To be classified as held for sale, the following criteria must be met:

- The asset must be available for sale in its present condition

- The sale must be highly probable

- Management must be committed to the sale

- The asset should be actively marketed at a reasonable price

- The sale must be expected within a year

If the criteria are met:

- The asset should be measured at the lower of carrying amount and fair value less costs to sell.

- If the asset is measured using a revaluation model then it should be revalued to fair value before being classified as held for sale.

- The asset will be held as a current asset

- No further depreciation is charged.

## IAS 41 Agriculture

Definition

A **biological asset** is a '**living plant or animal**' (IAS 41, para 5).

**Agricultural produce** is the '**harvested product of the entity's biological assets**' (IAS 41, para 5).

The key rules from the standard are:

- Biological assets are initially measured at fair value less estimated costs to sell.

- At each reporting date, biological assets are revalued to fair value less costs to sell.

- At the date of harvest, agricultural produce should be recognised and measured at fair value less estimated costs to sell. It is then accounted for under IAS 2 Inventories.

## IAS 2 Inventories

Inventories are assets that the entity sells in the ordinary course of business (plus any associated raw materials and work in progress).

Inventories are measured at '**the lower of cost and net realisable value**' (IAS 2, para 9):

- **Cost** includes the purchase price and any other directly attributable costs.
- **Net realisable value** is the expected selling price, less estimated costs of completion and sale.

Recent examination questions include:

- March/June 2016 – Emcee
- June 2015 – Klancet
- December 2014 – Kayte

**6**

# Foreign currency in individual financial statements

**In this chapter**

- Functional currency.
- Translation rules.

## Functional currency

Functional currency is '**the currency of the primary economic environment where an entity operates**' (IAS 21, para 8).

Factors used to determine a functional currency are as follows:

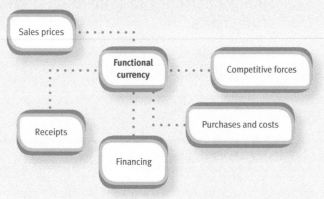

A subsidiary that operates with little autonomy will most likely have the same functional currency as its parent.

## Chapter 6

## Translation rules

**Overseas transactions**

**Initial transaction**
Translate into functional currency using the spot/historic rate.

**Settlement**
Translate the settlement into functional currency using the spot/historic rate.

**If unsettled**
The treatment depends on whether the overseas item is monetary.

**If monetary**
E.g. receivables, payables, loans
Retranslate at the closing rate of exchange.

**If non-monetary**
E.g. PPE, inventories
Do not retranslate.
However, if held under a fair value model, the fair value will need to be translated when determined.

Exam Focus

Recent examination questions on this topic include:

- September/December 2016 – Suntory
- June 2014 – Aspire

# 7

## Leases

In this chapter

- IFRS 16 Leases.
- Lessee accounting.
- Lessor accounting.
- Sale and leaseback.

## IFRS 16 Leases

**Definition**

A **lease** is a contract that conveys the right to use an underlying asset for a period of time in exchange for consideration.

The **lessor** is the entity that provides the right-of-use asset and, in exchange, receives consideration.

The **lessee** is the entity that obtains use of the right-of-use asset and, in exchange, transfers consideration.

### Identifying a lease

A contract contains a lease if it conveys the right to control the use of an identified asset for a period of time in exchange for consideration. For this to be the case, the contract must give the customer:

- the right to substantially all of the economic benefits from use of the identified asset, and

- the right to direct the use of the identified asset

## Lessee accounting

### Initial treatment

Except for the exceptions noted later, the lessee should recognise a lease liability and a right-of-use asset at the commencement of the lease:

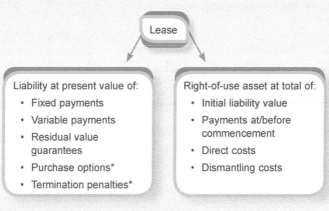

Lease

Liability at present value of:
- Fixed payments
- Variable payments
- Residual value guarantees
- Purchase options*
- Termination penalties*

Right-of-use asset at total of:
- Initial liability value
- Payments at/before commencement
- Direct costs
- Dismantling costs

* Include if reasonably certain to be incurred

## Subsequent treatment

- The carrying amount of the lease liability is increased by the interest charge. This interest is also recorded in the statement of profit or loss. The carrying amount of the lease liability is reduced by cash repayments.

- The right-of-use asset is measured using the cost model (unless another measurement model is chosen). This means it is measured at its initial cost less accumulated depreciation and impairment losses.

## Exceptions

The lessee can choose to recognise the lease payments in profit or loss on a straight line basis if the lease is

- short-term (less than 12 months at the inception date), or

- of a low value.

## Lessor accounting

### Lease classifications

Leases must be classified at inception as either a finance lease or an operating lease:

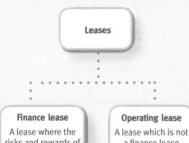

```
                    Leases

    Finance lease              Operating lease
    A lease where the          A lease which is not
    risks and rewards of       a finance lease
    ownership transfer
    to the lessee
```

IFRS 16 gives the following indications that the risks and rewards of ownership have transferred to the lessee:

- Ownership is transferred at the end of the lease
- The lessee has the option to purchase the asset at the end of the lease term for less than fair value
- The lessee can continue to lease the asset at the end of the lease term for less than market rents
- The lease term is for the major part of the asset's life
- The present value of the minimum lease payments are substantially all of the fair value of the leased asset.

## Lessor accounting treatment

Under a finance lease, the lessor must:

- derecognise the leased asset
- recognise a lease receivable at the present value of the minimum lease payments plus the estimated unguaranteed residual value of the asset
- recognise income on the lease receivable using the rate implicit in the lease.

Under an operating lease, the lessor must:

- continue to recognise and depreciate the leased asset
- recognise lease rental income in profit or loss on a straight line basis.

## Sale and leaseback

The treatment of a sale and leaseback depends on whether the 'sale' represents the satisfaction of a performance obligation (as per IFRS 15 Revenue from Contracts with Customers).

|  | Transfer is not a sale | Transfer is a sale |
|---|---|---|
| Seller-lessee | Continue to recognise asset<br><br>Recognise a financial liability equal to proceeds received. | Derecognise the asset.<br><br>Recognise a right-of-use asset as the proportion of the previous carrying amount that relates to the rights retained.<br><br>Recognise a lease liability.<br><br>A profit or loss on disposal will arise. |
| Buyer-lessor | Do not recognise the asset<br><br>Recognise a financial asset equal to transfer proceeds. | Account for the asset purchase.<br><br>Account for the lease by applying lessor accounting requirements. |

**Exam focus**

Recent examination questions include:

- June 2015 – Kutchen
- June 2013 – Janne

# 8

## Employee benefits

**In this chapter**

- Overview.
- Pensions.
- Measurement of defined benefit pension assets and liabilities.
- Other employee benefits.

## Overview

- Pension schemes are an important area that is examined frequently.
- You must be prepared to deal with computational and discussion elements.

## Pensions

**Types of pension scheme**

**Defined contribution**

An entity pays fixed contributions and will have no legal or constructive obligation to pay further contributions if the fund does not hold sufficient assets to pay all employee benefits.

**Defined benefit**

A pension scheme that is not a defined contribution scheme.

For a defined contribution scheme, contributions payable are recognised as an expense in profit or loss.

The accounting treatment of a defined benefit scheme is covered in more detail in the next section.

## Measurement of defined benefit pension assets and liabilities

IAS 19 requires that:

- **plan assets** are measured at their fair value at the end of the reporting period
- **plan liabilities** are measured on an actuarial basis and are discounted to present value at the end of the reporting period.

The net liability (deficit) or net asset (surplus) is reported at each reporting date.

Note that where there is a net asset, the **asset ceiling test** may apply. This restricts the value of the net asset reported to the extent that it is regarded as recoverable.

### Defined benefit plan movement

The following proforma shows the movement on the defined benefit deficit (or a surplus) over a reporting period:

|  | $ |
|---|---|
| Net deficit/(asset) brought forward (Obligation bfd – assets bfd) | X/(X) |
|  |  |
| Net interest component | X/(X) |
| Service cost component | X |
| Contributions into plan | (X) |
| Benefits paid | – |
|  | ——— |
|  | X/(X) |
|  |  |
| Remeasurement component (bal. fig) | X/(X) |
|  | ——— |
| Net deficit/(asset) carried forward (Obligation cfd – assets cfd) | X/(X) |
|  | ——— |

### Definitions

- **Current service cost** is the '**increase in the present value of the defined benefit obligation resulting from employee service in the current period**' (IAS 19, para 8). This is part of the service cost component.

- **Past service cost** is the '**change in present value of the defined benefit obligation for employee service in prior periods resulting from a plan amendment or curtailment in the current period**' (IAS 19, para 8). This is part of the service cost component.

- A **curtailment** arises when there is a significant reduction in the number of employees covered by a plan. Any gain or loss on curtailment is part of the service cost component.

- A **settlement** arises when an entity enters into a transaction to terminate all or part of the benefits due to one or more employees under a plan. This is part of the service cost component.

- **Net interest component** is the change in measurement in both the plan obligation and plan assets due to the passage of time. It is calculated by applying the discount rate for the liability to the net liability (or asset) at the start of the reporting period. This is charged (or credited) to profit or loss.

- **The remeasurement component** arises due to differences between assumptions and estimates made when accounting for the defined benefit plan, and what has actually happened. The remeasurement component is taken to other comprehensive income.

### Recognising the amounts in the financial statements

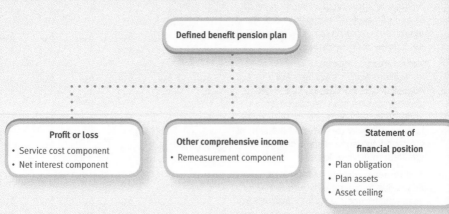

## Other employee benefits

**Other long-term employee benefits**
- Account for in similar way to defined benefit pension plans – spread cost over service period

**Short-term employee benefits**
- Normal accruals accounting
- Cumulating or non-cumulating

**Termination benefits**
- Recognise when an obligation or when related restructuring costs recognised

## Exam focus

Recent exam questions include:

- September/December 2016 – Zippy
- September/December 2015 – Bubble
- June 2015 – Kutchen

# 9

## Share-based payment

In this chapter

- Overview.
- Accounting for share-based payments.

## Overview

A share-based payment is where an entity receives goods or services in exchange for shares, share options or cash based on a share price.

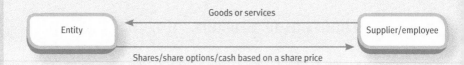

### Recognising the expense

The expense of a share-based payment scheme is recognised in profit or loss over the vesting period based on the number of share-based payments expected to vest. If there are no vesting conditions, then the expense is recognised immediately.

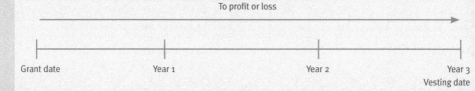

**Grant date**: the date a share-based payment transaction is entered into.

**Vesting date**: the date on which the cash or equity instruments can be received by the other party to the agreement.

There are two types of share based payment transactions:

(1) **Equity-settled** share based payment transactions where a company receives goods or services in exchange for equity instruments (e.g. shares or share options).

(2) **Cash-settled** share based payment transactions, where a company receives goods and services in exchange for a cash amount paid based on its share price.

## Accounting for share-based payments

### Equity-settled share-based payments

The value of an equity-settled share-based payment transaction is determined as follows:

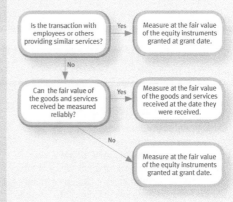

This should be recognised in profit or loss over the vesting period based on the number of shares or options that are expected to vest.

The accounting entry posted at each reporting date is:

Dr Profit or loss

Cr Equity

## Modifications

If a modification to an equity-settled sharebased payment scheme occurs:

- the entity continues to recognise the grant date fair value of the equity instruments in profit or loss

- the entity also recognises an extra expense based on the difference between the fair value of the new arrangement and the fair value of the original arrangement (the incremental fair value) between the date of the change and the vesting date.

## Cancellations

If an entity cancels or settles a share option scheme before the vesting date:

- The entity immediately recognises the amount that would otherwise have been recognised for services received over the vesting period (an acceleration of vesting)

- Any payment made to employees up to the fair value of the equity instruments at cancellation is accounted for as a deduction from equity.

- Any payment made to employees in excess of the fair value of the equity instruments at cancellation is accounted for as an expense in profit or loss.

## Cash-settled share-based payments

Cash-settled schemes are often referred to as share-appreciation rights (SARs).

There are two key differences between the accounting treatment of SARs and an equity-settled share-based payment scheme:

- For a cash scheme, the expense is valued using the fair value of the SARs at the reporting date.

- The accounting entry required is:

    Dr Profit or loss

    Cr Liabilities

### Exam focus

Recent examination questions include:

- June 2015 – Yanong
- December 2014 – Joey

# 10

## Provisions and events after the reporting period

**In this chapter**

- IAS 37 Provisions, contingent liabilities and contingent assets.
- IAS 10 Events after the reporting period.

## IAS 37 Provisions, contingent liabilities and contingent assets

### Definition

- A provision is '**a liability of uncertain timing or amount**' (IAS 37, para 10).

- A contingent liability is a possible obligation whose existence will be confirmed by uncertain future events outside of the entity's control.

- A contingent asset is a possible asset whose existence will be confirmed by uncertain future events outside of the entity's control.

**Provisions**

**Recognition**

Recognise when:

- an entity has a present obligation (legal or constructive) as a result of a past event,

- it is probable that an outflow of economic benefits will be required, and

- a reliable estimate can be made.

**Measurement**

- The amount recognised should be the **best estimate** of the expenditure required to settle the obligation.

- Where the time value of money is material, the provision should be discounted to present value.

**Specific guidance**

**Future operating losses**
- Provisions should not be recognised for future operating losses.

**Onerous contracts**
- Provisions should be recognised for the obligation under the contract.

**Restructuring**
- Provisions can only be recognised where an entity has a constructive obligation to carry out the restructuring.
- A constructive obligation arises when there is a detailed formal plan and the plan has been announced to those affected.

**Contingent liabilities** should not be recognised. They should be disclosed unless the possibility of a transfer of economic benefits is remote.

**Contingent assets** should not be recognised. If the possibility of an inflow of economic benefits is probable they should be disclosed.

# IAS 10 Events after the reporting period

## Exam focus

Recent examination questions include:

- September/December 2015 – Gasnature
- June 2014 – Minco

# Financial instruments

In this chapter

- Definitions.
- Financial liabilities.
- Compound financial instruments.
- Financial assets.
- Financial asset impairments.
- Derecognition of financial instruments.
- Derivatives.
- Hedge accounting.
- Disclosure of financial instruments.

## Definitions

A financial instrument is '**any contract that gives rise to a financial asset of one entity and a financial liability or equity instrument of another entity**' (IAS 32, para 11).

A **financial asset** is any asset that is:

- 'cash
- an equity instrument of another entity
- a contractual right to receive cash or another financial asset from another entity
- a contractual right to exchange financial instruments with another entity under conditions that are potentially favourable' (IAS 32, para 11).

A **financial liability** is any liability that is a:

- 'contractual obligation to deliver cash or another financial asset to another entity
- contractual obligation to exchange financial instruments with another entity under conditions that are potentially unfavourable
- a contract that will or may be settled in the entity's own equity instruments and is a non-derivative for which the entity is or may be obliged to deliver a variable number of the entity's own equity instruments' (IAS 32, para 11).

An **equity instrument** is 'any contract that evidences a residual interest in the assets of an entity after deducting all of its liabilities' (IAS 32, para 11).

## Financial liabilities

### Initial recognition

At initial recognition, financial liabilities are measured at fair value.

- If the financial liability will be held at fair value through profit or loss, transaction costs should be expensed to the statement of profit or loss.

- If the financial liability will not be held at fair value through profit or loss, transaction costs should be deducted from its carrying amount.

### Subsequent treatment

The subsequent treatment of a financial liability is that they can be measured at either:

- amortised cost (most borrowings)

- fair value through profit or loss (liabilities held for trading).

## Compound financial instruments

A compound instrument is a financial instrument that has characteristics of both equity and liabilities. An example would be debt that can be redeemed either in cash or in equity shares.

IAS 32 requires compound financial instruments to be split into:

- a financial liability (the liability to repay the debt holder in cash)

- an equity instrument (the option to convert into shares).

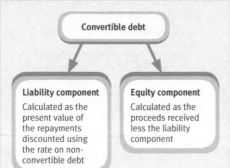

**Convertible debt**

**Liability component**
Calculated as the present value of the repayments discounted using the rate on non-convertible debt

**Equity component**
Calculated as the proceeds received less the liability component

## Financial assets

### Initial recognition

At initial recognition, financial assets are measured at fair value.

- If the financial asset will be held at fair value through profit or loss, transaction costs should be expensed to the statement of profit or loss.

- If the financial asset will not be held at fair value through profit or loss, transaction costs should be added to its carrying amount.

### Investments in equity

Investments in equity instruments (such as an investment in the ordinary shares of another entity) are normally measured at fair value through profit or loss.

It is possible to measure an equity instrument at fair value through other comprehensive income, provided that:

- the equity instrument is not held for trading, and

- an irrevocable choice for this designation is made upon initial recognition of the asset.

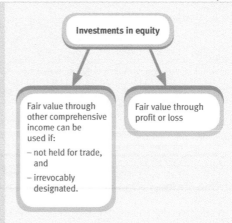

Investments in equity

Fair value through other comprehensive income can be used if:
– not held for trade, and
– irrevocably designated.

Fair value through profit or loss

### Investments in debt

Financial assets that are debt instruments can be measured in one of three ways:

1. An investment in a debt instrument is measured at amortised cost if:

- The financial asset is held within a business model whose aim is to collect the contractual cash flows.

- The contractual terms of the financial asset give rise to cash flows that are solely payments of principal and interest on the principal amount outstanding.

2. An investment in a debt instrument is measured at fair value through other comprehensive income if:

- The financial asset is held within a business model whose objective is achieved by both collecting contractual cash flows and selling financial assets.

- The contractual terms of the financial asset give rise to cash flows that are solely payments of principal and interest on the principal amount outstanding.

3. An investment in a debt instrument that is not measured at amortised cost or fair value through other comprehensive income will be measured at fair value through profit or loss.

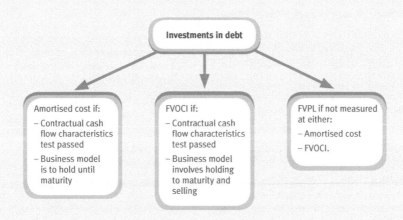

## Financial asset impairments

The impairment rules in IFRS 9 apply to debt instruments measured at amortised cost or at fair value through other comprehensive income.

For financial assets within the scope of the impairment rules, entities must calculate a loss allowance.

Increases and decreases in the loss allowance are charged to profit or loss.

This loss allowance must be equal to:

- **12 month expected credit losses** if credit risk has not increased significantly

- **Lifetime expected credit losses** if credit risk has increased significantly.

### Definitions

**Credit loss:** the present value of the difference between the contractual cash flows due to an entity and the cash flows that it expects to receive.

**Expected credit loss:** the weighted average credit losses.

**Lifetime expected credit losses:** The expected credit losses that result from all possible default events.

**12 month expected credit losses:** The proportion of the lifetime expected credit losses that arise from default events within 12 months of the reporting date.

## Derecognition of financial instruments

A financial asset should be derecognised if one of the following has occurred:

- the contractual rights to the cash flows of the financial asset have expired.
- the financial asset has been sold and substantially all the **risks and rewards of ownership** have been transferred from the seller to the buyer.

A financial liability should be derecognised when the obligation specified in the contract is discharged, cancelled or has expired.

The accounting treatment of derecognition is as follows:

- The difference between the carrying amount of the asset or liability and the amount received or paid should be recognised in profit or loss for the period.
- For investments in equity instruments held at fair value through other comprehensive income, the cumulative gains and losses recognised in other comprehensive income are **not recycled** to profit or loss on disposal.
- For investments in debt instruments held at fair value through other comprehensive income, the cumulative gains and losses recognised in other comprehensive income **are recycled** to profit or loss on disposal.

## Derivatives

A derivative is a financial instrument with the following characteristics:

(a) Its value changes in response to an underlying variable.

(b) It requires little or no initial investment.

(c) It is settled at a future date.

Derivatives are measured at fair value through profit or loss.

## Hedge accounting

Types of hedge accounting

**A fair value hedge**

'A hedge of the exposure to changes in fair value of a recognised asset or liability or an unrecognised firm commitment that is attributable to a particular risk and could affect profit or loss (or other comprehensive income for equity investments measured at fair value through other comprehensive income)' (IFRS 9, para 6.5.2).

**A cash flow hedge**

'A hedge of the exposure to variability in cash flows that is attributable to a particular risk associated with a recognised asset or liability or a highly probable forecast transaction and that could affect profit or loss' (IFRS 9, para 6.5.2).

Derivatives introduce volatility into profit or loss. Hedge accounting is a method of managing this by designating one or more hedging instruments so that their change in fair value is offset, in whole or in part, by the change in fair value or cash flows of a hedged item.

### Criteria

Under IFRS 9, hedge accounting rules can only be applied if the hedging relationship meets the following:

- The hedge consists of eligible hedging instruments and hedged items.
- At the inception of the hedge formal documentation identifies the hedged item and the hedging instrument.
- The hedging relationship is effective.
- If the hedged item is a forecast transaction, then the transaction must be highly probable.

A hedging relationship is effective if the following three criteria are met:

1. 'There is an economic relationship between the hedged item and the hedging instrument.

2. The effect of credit risk does not dominate the value changes that result from that economic relationship.

3. The hedge ratio of the hedging relationship is the same as that resulting from the quantity of the hedged item that the entity actually hedges and the quantity of the hedging instrument that the entity actually uses to hedge that quantity of hedged item' (IFRS 9, para 6.4.1).

### Accounting treatment of a fair value hedge

At the reporting date:

- the hedging instrument will be remeasured to fair value
- the carrying amount of the hedged item will be adjusted for the change in fair value since the inception of the hedge.

The gain (or loss) on the hedging instrument and the loss (or gain) on the hedged item will be recorded:

- in profit or loss in most cases, but
- in other comprehensive income if the hedged item is an investment in equity that is measured at fair value through other comprehensive income.

### Accounting treatment of a cash flow hedge

For cash flow hedges, the hedging instrument will be remeasured to fair value at the reporting date.

- The gain or loss is recognised in other comprehensive income.
- However, if the gain or loss on the hedging instrument since the inception of the hedge is greater than the loss or gain on the hedged item then the **excess** gain or loss on the instrument must be recognised in profit or loss.

### Discontinuing hedge accounting

An entity must cease hedge accounting if any of the following occur:

- The hedging instrument expires or is exercised, sold or terminated.
- The hedge no longer meets the hedging criteria.
- A forecast future transaction that qualified as a hedged item is no longer highly probable.

The discontinuance should be accounted for prospectively (entries posted to date are not reversed).

## Disclosure of financial instruments

IFRS 7 provides the disclosure requirements for financial instruments.

The main disclosures required are:

1. Information about the significance of financial instruments for an entity's financial position and performance.

2. Information about the nature and extent of risks arising from financial instruments.

## Exam focus

Recent examination questions include:

- September/December 2015 – Gasnature
- December 2014 – Coatmin

## chapter 12

## Tax

**In this chapter**

- Introduction to taxation.
- Deferred tax.
- Calculating deferred tax.
- Accounting for deferred tax.
- Specific scenarios.

## Introduction to taxation

There are two elements to tax that an entity has to deal with:

**Current tax** – the amount payable to the tax authorities in relation to the trading activities of the current period.

**Deferred tax** – an accounting measure used to match the tax effects of transactions with their accounting treatment.

In summary, the tax expense for an entity is calculated as follows:

Tax expense = current tax +/– movement in deferred tax

## Deferred tax

According to the accruals concept, the tax effect of a transaction should be reported in the same accounting period as the transaction itself.

Deferred tax is calculated on temporary differences between the accounting and tax treatment of a transaction.

A **temporary difference** is the difference between the carrying amount of an asset or liability and its tax base.

Examples of temporary differences include (but are not restricted to):

- Tax deductions for the cost of non-current assets that have a different pattern to the write off of the asset in the financial statements.
- Assets are revalued upwards in the financial statements, but no adjustment is made for tax purposes.
- Development costs are capitalised and amortised to profit or loss in future periods, but were deducted for tax purposes as incurred.

## Calculating deferred tax

The first step is to determine the temporary differences:

- If the carrying amount exceeds the tax base, the temporary difference is said to be a taxable temporary difference (a liability).
- If the tax base exceeds the carrying amount, the temporary difference is a deductible temporary difference (an asset).

The tax rate in force (or expected to be in force) when the asset is realised or the liability is settled is applied to the temporary difference to calculate the deferred tax balance.

This rate must be based on legislation enacted or substantively enacted by the reporting date.

Deferred tax assets and liabilities are **not** discounted to present value.

## Accounting for deferred tax

The entry to profit or loss and other comprehensive income in respect of deferred tax is the difference between the net liability/asset at the beginning of the year and the net liability/asset at the end of the year:

- If the item giving rise to the deferred tax is dealt with in profit or loss, the related deferred tax should also be presented in profit or loss.

- If the item giving rise to the deferred tax is dealt with in other comprehensive income, the related deferred tax should be recorded in other comprehensive income.

## Specific scenarios

### Share option schemes

The amount of tax relief granted is based on the intrinsic value of the options (the difference between the market price of the shares and the exercise price of the option) at the exercise date. This delayed tax relief gives rise to a deferred tax asset.

### Unused tax losses

Where an entity has unused tax losses, IAS 12 allows a deferred tax asset to be recognised to the extent that it is probable that future taxable profits will be available against which the unused tax losses can be utilised.

## Business combinations

A business combination has deferred tax consequences:

- The identifiable net assets of the acquired subsidiary are consolidated at fair value but the tax base derives from the values in the subsidiary's individual financial statements. A temporary difference is created, giving rise to deferred tax in the consolidated financial statements.

- Provisions for unrealised profits reduce the carrying amount of inventory in the consolidated financial statements but the tax base is its cost in the individual financial statements. A temporary difference is created, giving rise to a deferred tax asset in the consolidated financial statements.

Goodwill itself does not give rise to deferred tax because IAS 12 specifically excludes it.

### Exam focus

Recent examination questions include:

- September/December 2015 – Chemclean
- June 2014 – Aspire

# Segment reporting

In this chapter

- IFRS 8 Operating segments.

# IFRS 8 Operating segments

IFRS 8 Operating segments requires an entity to disclose information about each of its operating segments.

Definition

An **operating segment** is a component of an entity:

- that engages in business activities

- whose operating results are regularly reviewed by the entity's chief operating decision maker

- that has discrete financial information available.

## Aggregation

Two or more operating segments can be reported as a single operating segment provided that they have similar economic characteristics, and they are similar in terms o

- the products or services they sell

- production processes

- types of customers

- distribution methods.

## Reporting thresholds

An entity must separately report information about an operating segment that meets any of the following quantitative thresholds:

- 'its reported revenue, both sales to external customers and inter segmen sales, is 10 per cent or more of the combined revenue of all operating segments

- its reported profit or loss is 10 per cent or more of the greater, in absolute amount, of:
  - the combined reported profit of all operating segments that did not report a loss and
  - the combined reported loss of all operating segments that reported a loss.
- its assets are 10 per cent or more of the combined assets of all operating segments' (IFRS 8, para 13).

At least 75% of the entity's external revenue should be included in reportable segments. This means that other segments might need to be identified as reportable segments until this 75% threshold is reached.

## Disclosures

IFRS 8 requires detailed disclosures, including:

- factors used to identify the entity's reportable segments
- the types of products and services sold by each reportable segment

For each reportable segment an entity should report:

- a measure of profit or loss
- a measure of total assets
- a measure of total liabilities (if this amount is used in decision making).

Recent examination questions include:

- June 2015 – Klancet

## Related parties

In this chapter

- Related parties.
- Related party disclosures.

# Related parties

## Exam Focus

- Related party transactions are important as they can affect the performance and position of an entity.

- In the exam you may have to determine related party relationships and transactions.

## Definition

IAS 24 Related Party Disclosures says that a person, or member of their close family, is related to the reporting entity if they:

- have control or joint control over the entity

- have significant influence over the reporting entity

- are a member of key management personnel of the entity or its parent.

Two entities are related if:

- they are parents and subsidiaries within the same group

- one entity is an associate or joint venture of the other

- a person (or a member of their close family) who is a related party of one of the entities has control over the other

- a person who has control over one of the entities also has significant influence over the other entity or is a member of its (or its parent's) key management personnel.

## Summary

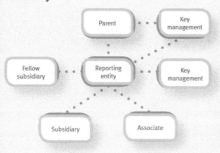

A **related party transaction** is the '**transfer of resources, services or obligations between related parties regardless of whether a price is charged**' (IAS 24, para 6).

## Related party disclosures

- Relationships between parents and subsidiaries.

- The name of the parent and the ultimate controlling party (if different).

- Key management personnel compensation.

- For related party transactions that have occurred disclosures should include:

  (a) the amount of the transactions

  (b) the amount of outstanding balances and their terms

  (c) allowances for doubtful debts relating to the outstanding balances

  (d) the expense recognised in the period in respect of irrecoverable or doubtful debts.

## Exam Focus

Recent examination questions include:

- September/December 2016 – Suntory
- December 2014 – Coatmin

# 15

## Adoption of International Financial Reporting Standards

**In this chapter**

- IFRS 1 First time adoption of International Financial Reporting Standards.

## IFRS 1 First time adoption of International Financial Reporting Standards

This standard sets out the procedures to be followed in adopting IFRS Standards for the first time.

**Definition**

IFRS 1 defines the **date of transition** as the beginning of the earliest period for which an entity presents full comparative information in its first financial statements prepared under IFRS Standards.

| 1/1/X0 | 31/12/X0 | 31/12/X1 |
|---|---|---|
| The date of transition to IFRS (The first day of the comparative period) | Comparative figures for first set of published IFRS financial statements | First set of published IFRS financial statements |

## Chapter 15

## Adoption of IFRS Standards

IFRS 1 states that the opening IFRS statement of financial position at the date of transition must:

- recognise all assets and liabilities required by IFRS Standards
- not recognise assets and liabilities not permitted by IFRS Standards
- reclassify all assets, liabilities and equity components in accordance with IFRS Standards
- measure all assets and liabilities in accordance with IFRS Standards.

Gains and losses arising on transition to IFRS Standards are recorded in retained earnings.

## Practical factors

Before adopting a new set of accounting standards, an entity should consider the following:

- Bonuses and performance related pay – impact of profit changes?
- IT systems – will they require updating or replacing?
- Covenants on loans – will they be breached?
- Earnings per share – will it reduce?
- Perception – will analysts view the move positively?
- Staff knowledge – is it sufficient?

### The benefits of convergence

There are a number of potential benefits from the worldwide convergence with International Financial Reporting Standards:

- Investors would be able to compare entities more easily

- Access to international finance would be easier

- Multi-national entities would save time and money when producing consolidated financial statements.

Exam focus

Recent examination questions include:

- March/June 2016 – Pod

# Specialised entities and specialised transactions

In this chapter

- Not for profit entities.
- Small and medium-sized entities.
- Entity reconstruction schemes.

## Not for profit entities

### Definition

A **not-for-profit entity** is one that does not carry on its activities for the purposes of profit or gain to particular persons, including its owners or members; and does not distribute its profits or assets to particular persons, including its owners or members.

The main types of not-for-profit entity are:

- clubs and societies
- charities
- public sector organisations.

### Objectives of not-for-profit entities

- The main objective of public sector organisations is to provide services to the general public.
- Most public sector organisations aim to provide value for money.
- Other not-for-profit entities include charities, clubs and societies whose objective is to carry out the activities for which they were created.

### Assessing performance in not-for-profit entities

- It can be difficult to monitor and evaluate the success of a not-for-profit organisation as the focus is not on profit
- The success of the organisation should be measured against the key indicators that reflect the visions and values of the organisation.

# Small and medium sized entities

## Definition

A small and medium sized entity (SME) is an entity that:

(1) does not have public accountability and

(2) publishes general purpose financial statements for external users.

## The problems of accounting for SMEs

- IFRS Standards are complex. Compliance with these brings a large reporting burden on the entity.

- The main users of small company financial statements are normally the tax authorities, lenders and the owner/managers themselves. The recognition and measurement criteria used by large companies may not be appropriate and may even be unhelpful to the users.

## IFRS for SMEs Standard

This is a simplified, stand-alone set of accounting principles that are appropriate for smaller, non-listed entities. It is based on full IFRS Standards as far as practicable.

In comparison with full IFRS Standards, the IFRS for SMEs Standard:

- removes choices of accounting treatment such as the revaluation model for intangible assets.

- eliminates topics that are not generally relevant, such as requirements relating to earnings per share, interim reporting and segmental reporting

- simplifies recognition and measurement, for example by requiring all research and development costs to be expensed as incurred.

Recent examination questions include:

- December 2010 – IFRS for SME

## Entity reconstruction schemes

Key characteristics of an entity that may benefit from a reconstruction scheme:

- accumulated trading losses
- arrears of unpaid interest
- no payment of equity dividends for several years
- market value of equity shares below the nominal value
- lack of investor and market confidence.

A reconstruction of the entity may involve one or more of the following procedures:

- write off the accumulated losses
- write off arrears of repayment of loan finance
- write down the nominal value of the equity capital.

## Capital reduction scheme

Using this scheme, an entity may:

- write off unpaid equity capital, for example, on partly paid shares
- write off any equity capital which is lost or not represented by available assets
- write off any paid up equity capital which is in excess of requirements.

This scheme does not really affect creditors as the equity holders have reduced their capital stake in the entity, either by reducing the nominal value of the shares in issue, or by reducing the total number of shares in issue, or a combination of both.

This scheme is normally regulated by formalised procedures detailed in law.

## Reconstruction schemes

Reconstruction schemes extend the principles of the capital reduction schemes by including the various creditors within the scheme. Typically, they will surrender their current legal rights (e.g repayment and enforcement of collateral) in exchange for new rights in an entity likely to continue as a going concern.

### External reconstruction schemes

Such schemes normally involve the assets and liabilities of the current entity being transferred to a new entity on an agreed basis. Typically, this will require information regarding the following:

- details of purchase or transfer values
- details of sale, transfer, write-off or realisation of the assets and liabilities, which may lead to a profit or loss on realisation for the vendor
- how repayment or settlement of capital of the selling entity is to be arranged.

Recent examination questions include:

- December 2011 – Decany

# Non-financial reporting

In this chapter

- Overview.
- Stakeholders.
- Sustainability reporting.
- Environmental reporting.
- Social reporting.
- The International Integrated Reporting Council (IIRC).
- Management commentary.

## Overview

- Questions set on this topic are likely to be a mixture of discussion or scenario based.

- Make sure that you understand the reasons behind reporting as well as the requirements for it.

- Large businesses are accepting the idea that they are responsible to a wider group of stakeholders, rather than just their shareholders.

- There is a demand for information on the environmental and social impact of companies' activities.

- Increasingly, companies are considering the environmental and social impact of their actions when making business decisions, sometimes called **corporate citizenship**.

## Stakeholders

The stakeholders of a business are as follows:

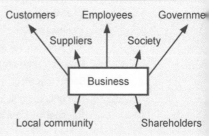

The needs of stakeholders may be different.

# Sustainability reporting

**Sustainability** is the process of conducting business in such a way that it enables an entity to meet its present needs without compromising the ability of future generations to meet their needs.

- In a corporate context, sustainability means that a business entity must attempt to reduce its environmental impact through more efficient use of natural resources and improving environmental practices.

- Sustainability reports include highlights of non-financial performance such as environmental, social and economic reports during the accounting period.

- There is no framework for sustainability reporting in IFRS, so this reporting is voluntary.

# Environmental reporting

**Environmental reporting** is the disclosure of information in the published annual report or elsewhere, of the effect that the operations of the business have on the natural environment.

Most environmental reports take the form of a combined statement of policy and review of activity. They cover issues such as:

- waste management

- pollution

- intrusion into the landscape

- the effect of an entity's activities upon wildlife

- use of energy, and

- the benefits to the environment of the entity's products and services.

## Social reporting

Definition

**Corporate Social Responsibility** is the continuing commitment by business to behave ethically and contribute to economic development while improving the quality of life of the workforce and their families as well as of the local community and society at large.

### Contents of social reports

- The Institute of Social and Ethical Accountability suggest the following should be included.

  - Information about relationships with stakeholders, e.g. employee numbers, wages and salaries, provision of facilities for customers and information about involvement with local charities.

  - Information about the accountability of the entity, e.g. sickness leave, accident rates, noise levels, numbers of disabled employees.

  - Information about dialogue with stakeholders, e.g. the way in which the entity consults with stakeholders and its performance in meeting stakeholder needs.

## The International Integrated Reporting Council (IIRC)

The IIRC was created to respond to the need for a concise, clear, comprehensive and comparable integrated reporting framework:

- The IIRC define an integrated report (IR) as 'a concise communication about how an organisation's strategy, governance, performance and prospects, in the context of its external environment, lead to the creation of value in the short, medium and long term'.

- The IR Framework establishes 'guiding principles' and 'content elements' that govern the overall content of an integrated report. This will help organisations to report their value creation in ways that are understandable and useful to the users.

The IR Framework says that an integrated report should include all of the following content elements:

- **Organisational overview and external environment** – 'What does the organisation do and what are the circumstances under which it operates?'

- **Governance** – 'How does the organisation's governance structure support its ability to create value in the short, medium and long term?'

- **Opportunities and risks** – 'What are the specific opportunities and risks that affect the organisation's ability to create value over the short, medium and long term, and how is the organisation dealing with them?'

- **Strategy and resource allocation** – 'Where does the organisation want to go and how does it intend to get there?'

- **Business model** – 'What is the organisation's business model and to what extent is it resilient?'

- **Performance** – 'To what extent has the organisation achieved its strategic objectives and what are its outcomes in terms of effects on the capitals?'

- **Future outlook** – 'What challenges and uncertainties is the organisation likely to encounter in pursuing its strategy, and what are the potential implications for its business model and future performance?'

- **Basis of presentation** – 'How does the organisation determine what matters to include in the integrated report and how are such matters quantified or evaluated?'

Including this content will help companies shift the focus of their reporting from historical financial performance to longer-term value creation.

# Management commentary

Definition

Management commentary is a narrative report that provides a context within which to interpret financial statements.

Practice Statement 1, issued in December 2010, is a non-binding framework for entities to follow when they prepare management commentary information.

The commentary should enable users to understand:

- the nature of the business
- management's objectives, and strategies for meeting those objectives
- the entity's most significant financial and non-financial resources
- the entity's most significant risks

- the entity's most significant relationships, particularly with stakeholders
- the results of operations
- the critical performance measures and indicators used by management.

Exam focus

Recent examination questions include:

- September/December 2016 – Sanchera
- March/June 2016 – Weston
- June 2015 – IAS1 and Integrated Reporting

# 18

## Current issues

### In this chapter

- What is a current issue?
- Studying current issues.

## What is a current issue?

According to the ACCA, a 'current issue' can include:

- recent IFRS Standards
- practice and regulatory issues
- proposed changes to IFRS Standards
- problems with existing IFRS Standards.

## Studying current issues

Further information about 'current issues' can be found in Chapter 18 of the Study Text.

The examiners have frequently emphasised the importance of wider reading.

- You should review relevant press article for current developments in corporate reporting.
- You should review the ACCA web site for articles relevant to your studies at: www.accaglobal.com.

There will always be an essay-style question in the examination. The question may include a computational element.

Recent examination questions include:

- September/December 2016 – Materiality and cash flow statements
- September/December 2015 – Revenue from contracts with customers
- June 2015 – IAS1 and Integrated Reporting

# Group accounting – basic groups

In this chapter

- Overview.
- IFRS 10 Consolidated financial statements.
- The acquisition method.
- Basic workings.
- Goodwill.
- Associates (IAS 28).
- Joint arrangements (IFRS 11).
- Disclosure of interests in other entities (IFRS 12).
- IAS 27 Separate financial statements.

## Overview

Exam focus

- Question one will always be on group accounting.

- Basic principles will enable you to get the easy marks in the question before attempting any of the trickier parts.

## IFRS 10 Consolidated Financial Statements

Definition

A **parent** is an entity that controls another entity.

A **subsidiary** is an entity that is controlled by a parent entity.

IFRS 10 says that an investor has control when it has:

- power over the investee

- exposure, or rights to, variable returns from involvement in the investee

- the ability to use power over the investee to affect the investor's returns.

An entity that is a parent is required to produce consolidated financial statements.

## The acquisition method

IFRS 3 applies to business combinations. A business combination is where an acquirer obtains control of a business.

- If the assets purchased are not a business, then the transaction is accounted for as an asset purchase

- If the assets purchased are a business then the acquisition method is applied.

The acquisition method has four requirements.

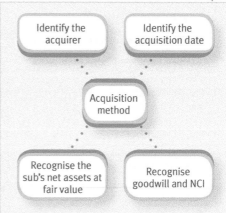

Identify the acquirer

Identify the acquisition date

Acquisition method

Recognise the sub's net assets at fair value

Recognise goodwill and NCI

## Basic workings

**SOFP – basic workings – overview**

**Consolidated statement of financial position**

| | |
|---|---|
| Goodwill (W3) | x |
| Assets (P + S) | x |
| | —— |
| Total assets | x |
| | —— |
| Share capital (P's only) | x |
| Other components of equity (W5) | x |
| Retained earnings (W5) | x |
| NCI (W4) | x |
| | —— |
| Total equity | x |
| | —— |
| Liabilities (P + S) | x |
| | —— |
| Total equity and liabilities | x |
| | —— |

Set out your workings as follows:

**W1 Group structure**

**W2 Net assets of each subsidiary**

| | At acquisition date $000 | At reporting date $000 |
|---|---|---|
| Equity share capital | X | X |
| Other components of equity | X | X |
| Retained earnings | X | X |
| Fair value adjustments | X /(X) | X /(X) |
| Post-acq'n accounting adjustments | | |
| e.g. PURP on sales made by S | | X /(X) |
| | X | X |
| | To W3 | |

| W3 Goodwill | |
|---|---|
| | $000 |
| FV of consideration | X |
| NCI at acquisition | X |
| | ___ |
| | X |
| FV of net assets at acquisition (W2) | (X) |
| | ___ |
| Goodwill at acquisition | X |
| | |
| Impairment to date | (X) |
| | ___ |
| Goodwill at reporting date | X |
| | ___ |

| W4 Non-controlling interest | |
|---|---|
| | $000 |
| NCI at acquisition (W3) | X |
| NCI% x post-acquisition reserves (W2) | X |
| Less: NCI% of goodwill impairment (W3) (FV method only) | (X) |
| | ___ |
| | X |
| | ___ |

| **W5 Group reserves** | | **Other components of equity** | |
|---|---|---|---|
| **Retained earnings** | | | |
| | | | $000 |
| | $000 | Parent company | X |
| Parent company (100%) | X | Subsidiary: Group share of | |
| Subsidiary: Group share of post acquisition retained earnings (W2) | X | post-acquisition other components of equity (W2) | X |
| Less goodwill impairment (W3)* | (X) | | —— |
| PURP if P is seller | (X) | | X |
| | —— | | —— |
| | X | | |
| | —— | | |

*P% only if FV method used

**Consolidated statement of profit or loss and other comprehensive income**

**Step 1: Group structure**

**Step 2: Set up the pro-forma**

| | $000 |
|---|---|
| Revenue (P + S) | X |
| Cost of sales (P + S) | (X) |
| | — |
| Gross profit | X |
| Operating costs (P + S) | (X) |
| | — |
| Operating profit | X |
| Finance costs (P + S) | (X) |
| | — |
| Profit before tax | X |
| Tax (P + S) | (X) |
| | — |
| Profit for the period | Y |

| | |
|---|---|
| Other comprehensive income (P + S) | X |
| | — |
| Total comprehensive income (TCI) | Z |
| | — |
| **Profit attributable to:** | |
| Equity holders of group (bal.) | X |
| Non-controlling interest (step 4) | X |
| | — |
| | Y |
| | — |
| **TCI attributable to:** | |
| Equity holders of group (bal.) | X |
| Non-controlling interest (step 4) | X |
| | — |
| | Z |
| | — |

### Step 3: Complete the pro-forma

Add together the parent and subsidiary's incomes and expenses and items of other comprehensive income on a line-by-line basis.

- If the subsidiary has been acquired mid-year, pro-rate the results of the subsidiary so that only post-acquisition incomes, expenses and other comprehensive income are consolidated.
- Eliminate intra-group incomes and expenses, unrealised profits on intra-group transactions, as well as any dividends received from the subsidiary.

**Step 4: Calculate the profit/TCI attributable to the non-controlling interest**

|  | Profit | TCI |
|---|---|---|
|  | $000 | $000 |
| Profit/TCI of the subsidiary for the year |  |  |
| (pro-rated for mid-year acquisition) | X | X |
| PURP (if S is the seller) | (X) | (X) |
| Excess depreciation/amortisation | (X) | (X) |
| Goodwill impairment (under FV model only) | (X) | (X) |
|  | ——— | ——— |
| × NCI % | X | X |
|  | ——— | ——— |
| Profit/TCI attributable to the NCI | X | X |

## Goodwill

When calculating goodwill purchase consideration is measured at fair value. The NCI at acquisition can be measured at:

- Fair value
- Its proportion of the subsidiary's net assets.

### Fair value method

If the NCI is valued at fair value at acquisition then:

- 'Full goodwill' (the group and the NCI's goodwill) is calculated
- The impairment losses must be allocated between the group and the NCI.

### Proportion of net assets method

If the NCI is valued at acquisition at its share of the subsidiary's net assets then only the group's goodwill is calculated.

When calculating an impairment loss under this method:

- Goodwill must be grossed up to include the NCI's share.
- Only the group's share of the impairment loss is recognised.

## Associates (IAS 28)

### Definition

- IAS 28 Accounting for Associates and Joint Ventures defines an associate as **'an entity over which the investor has significant influence'** (IAS 28, para 3).
- Significant influence is the power to participate in the financial and operating policy decisions of an entity.
- A holding of between 20% and 50% of the voting power is presumed to give significant influence.

### Accounting for associates

Associates are accounted for using the equity method.

**Statement of financial position**

| | $000 |
|---|---|
| Cost | X |
| Add: share of increase in net assets | X |
| Less: impairment losses | (X) |
| Investment in Associate | X |

**Profit or loss**

Include the group's share of the associate's **profit after tax less any impairment losses**.

# Joint arrangements (IFRS 11)

## Definition

Joint arrangements are defined as arrangements where '**two or more parties have joint control**' (IFRS 11, para 4). This exists when the relevant activities require unanimous consent.

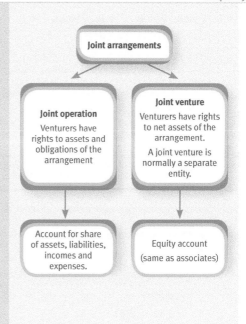

## Disclosure of interests in other entities (IFRS 12)

IFRS 12 outlines the disclosures required when one entity has an investment in another.

## IAS 27 Separate financial statements

IAS 27 applies when an entity has interests in subsidiaries, joint ventures or associates and it prepares separate non-consolidated financial statements.

In separate financial statements, investments in subsidiaries, joint ventures or associates can be accounted for in one of the following ways:

- cost
- in accordance with IFRS 9 Financial Instruments, or
- using the equity method.

## Exam focus

Recent examination questions include:

- September/December 2015 – Gasnatur
- June 2015 – Kutchen
- December 2014 – Joey

KAPLAN PUBLIS

# Complex groups

In this chapter

- Overview.
- Vertical group structures.
- Mixed (D-shaped) group structures.

## Overview

**Exam focus**

- These more complex situations may feature in the exam as part of the compulsory Q1.

## Vertical group structures

A vertical group will consist of an **indirectly controlled** subsidiary

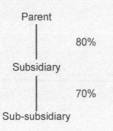

The group's effective shareholding in the sub-subsidiary is 56% (80% × 70%). This is used to calculate group reserves (W5).

The NCI's effective shareholding in the sub-subsidiary is 44% (100 − 56%). This is used to calculate the NCI reserve (W4).

When calculating goodwill in the sub-subsidiary in the above example, an **indirect holding adjustment** must be posted for 20% of the consideration paid by the subsidiary for the sub-subsidiary. The entry is:

Dr Non-controlling interest (W4)

Cr Goodwill (W3)

## Mixed (D-shaped) group structures

A mixed group contains a sub-subsidiary in which the parent has both a direct and an indirect shareholding.

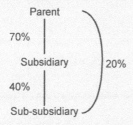

The group's effective shareholding in the sub-subsidiary is 48% (20% + (70% × 40%)). This is used to calculate group reserves (W5).

The NCI's effective shareholding is 52% (100 – 48%). This is used to calculate the NCI reserve (W4).

When calculating goodwill in the sub-subsidiary in the above example, an **indirect holding adjustment** must be posted for 30% of the consideration paid by the subsidiary for the sub-subsidiary. The entry is:

Dr Non-controlling interest (W4)

Cr Goodwill (W3)

**Exam focus**

Recent examination questions include:

- June 2013 – Trailer

# Change in a group structure

In this chapter

- Overview.
- Step acquisition.
- Disposal of subsidiaries where control is lost.
- Control to control scenarios.

## Overview

This chapter concerns the impact of different types of share purchases and share sales on the consolidated financial statements

## Step acquisition

A step acquisition occurs when the parent company acquires control over the subsidiary in stages. Acquisition accounting is only applied at the date when control is achieved.

At the date control is achieved:

(1) re-measure the previously held equity interest to fair value

(2) recognise any resulting gain or loss in profit or loss for the year

(3) calculate goodwill and the non-controlling interest.

For the purposes of the goodwill calculation use the following proforma:

|  | $000 |
| --- | --- |
| Fair value of previously held interest | X |
| Fair value of consideration for additional interest | X |
| NCI at acquisition | X |
|  | — |
|  | X |
| Less: FV of net assets at acquisition | (X) |
|  | — |
| Goodwill at acquisition | X |
|  | — |

## Disposal of subsidiaries where control is lost

If the sale of shares causes control over a subsidiary to be lost, then the treatment in the consolidated financial statements is as follows:

- Consolidate the incomes and expenses of the subsidiary up until the disposal date.
- On disposal of the subsidiary, derecognise its assets, liabilities, goodwill and non-controlling interest and calculate a profit or loss on disposal.
- Recognise any remaining investment in the shares of the former subsidiary at fair value and subsequently account for this under the relevant accounting standard.

- A holding of 20-50% of the shares would probably mean that the remaining investment is an associate, which should be accounted for using the equity method.
- A holding of less than 20% of the shares would probably mean that the remaining investment should be accounted for under IFRS 9 Financial Instruments.

The profit or loss on disposal is calculated as follows:

|  | $000 | $000 |
|---|---|---|
| Disposal proceeds | | X |
| Fair value of retained interest | | X |
| | | —— |
| | | X |
| Less interest in subsidiary disposed of: | | |
| Net assets of subsidiary at disposal date | X | |
| Goodwill at disposal date | X | |
| Less: Carrying amount of NCI at disposal date | (X) | |
| | —— | |
| | | (X) |
| | | —— |
| Profit/(loss) to the group | | X/(X) |
| | | —— |

If a subsidiary is acquired exclusively with a view to subsequent disposal and it meets the held for sale criteria in IFRS 5:

- it is presented in the financial statements as a disposal group classified as held for sale. This is achieved by amalgamating all its assets into one line item and all its liabilities into another

- it is measured, both on acquisition and at subsequent reporting dates, at fair value less costs to sell.

## Control to control scenarios

Share transactions that do not result in losing or gaining control include:

In such control-to-control scenarios:

- Goodwill is not recalculated
- No profit or loss arises
- Adjustments are made to the non-controlling interest and other components of equity.

Upon purchase of additional equity shares where control has already been acquired

|  | $000 |
|---|---|
| Cash paid by group to buy additional shares | (X) |

Decrease in NCI at transaction date:

$$CV \text{ of } NCI \times \frac{\text{reduction in NCI\%}}{\text{NCI\% pre-transaction}}$$   X

| Increase (decrease) in equity | X or (X) |
|---|---|

Upon disposal of equity shares where control has not been lost:

|  |  | $000 |
|---|---|---|
| Proceeds from shares sold by group |  | X |
| Net assets of sub | X |  |
| Goodwill of sub | X |  |
| Apply increase in NCI% | X | (X) |
| Increase (decrease) in equity |  | X or (X) |

**Exam focus**

Recent examination questions include:

Step acquisitions

- December 2014 – Joey

Disposal of subsidiaries

- September/December 2016 – Zippy
- June 2014 – Marchant

# Group accounting – foreign currency

In this chapter

- Overview.
- Foreign subsidiaries.
- Proformas.

## Overview

- This chapter deals with the consolidation of foreign subsidiaries.

- Make sure you study this carefully as there are a number of rules to remember.

## Foreign subsidiaries

If a company has foreign subsidiaries whose functional currency is their local currency, their financial statements must be translated into the parent's presentation currency.

- All **assets and liabilities** are translated into the group's presentation currency using the **closing rate** of exchange.

- **Goodwill** is treated as an asset of the subsidiary. It is calculated using the functional currency of the subsidiary. It is then translated using the closing rate for inclusion in the group accounts.

- **Income and expenses** must be translated at the average rate for the period.

- **Exchange differences** arising on consolidation are recognised in other comprehensive income. On disposal of the subsidiary, they are recycled to the statement of profit or loss.

- Exchange differences arise from:

  - the retranslation of the opening net assets using the the closing rate

  - retranslation of the the the profit for the year from the average rate (used in the statement of profit or loss) to the closing rate (for inclusion in the statement of financial position)

  - the retranslation of goodwill at each reporting date using the closing rate

## Proformas

### Opening net assets and profit

The exchange gains or losses arising on the translation of opening net assets and profit for the year are generally calculated together.

The proforma for calculating the current year exchange gain or loss on the translation of the opening net assets and profit is as follows:

|  | DN | Exchange Rate | $ |
|---|---|---|---|
| Opening net assets | X | Opening rate | X |
| Profit/(loss) for the year | X/(X) | Average rate | X/(X) |
| **Exchange gain/(loss)** | – | **Bal fig.** | X/(X) |
| Closing net assets | X | Closing rate | X |

## Goodwill translation

The proforma for calculating the current year exchange gain or loss on the retranslation of goodwill is as follows:

|  | DN | Exchange Rate | $ |
|---|---|---|---|
| Opening goodwill | X | Opening rate | X |
| Impairment loss in year | (X) | Average rate | (X) |
| **Exchange gain/(loss)** | – | **Bal fig.** | X/(X) |
| Closing goodwill | X | Closing rate | X |

Recent examination questions include:

- September/December 2015 – Bubble
- June 2014 – Aspire

# 23

## Group reorganisations and restructuring

### In this chapter

- Definitions.
- Reasons for reorganisations.
- Changes of ownership within a group.
- Reverse acquisitions.

## Definitions

Definition

A group reconstruction is any of the following.

- Transfer of ownership of a subsidiary from one group entity to another.

- Addition of a new parent entity.

- Transfer of ownership of a subsidiary to a new entity which is not a group entity but has the same shareholders as the group's parent.

- The combination into a group of two or more entities whose shareholders are the same before the combination.

- The acquisition of shares of another entity which then issues shares so that the acquired entity has control of the combined entity.

## Reasons for reorganisations

There are a number of reasons why a group may wish to reorganise.

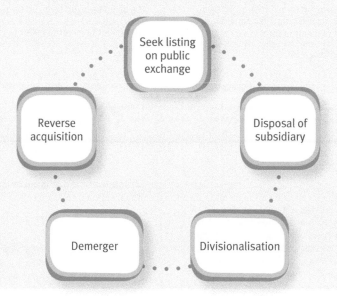

## Changes of ownership within a group

Changes of ownership within a group should not affect the consolidated accounts as no assets leave or are added to the group.

### Subsidiary moved up

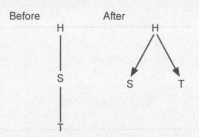

Before          After

This is usually dealt with by S paying a dividend in specie of the investment in T to H. Note that in some jurisdictions it is illegal for a parent to issue shares to a subsidiary so this reorganisation cannot be carried out by a share for share exchange.

### Accounting entries

S: Dr Retained earnings CR Investment in T

T: DR Investment in T CR Retained earnings

### Subsidiary moved down

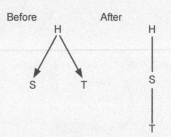

Before          After

This transaction can occur in one of two ways:

(1) S issues share to H in exchange for the shares in T.

(2) S pays cash to H for T. H may end up with a gain on disposal which must be eliminated in the group accounts.

## Subsidiary moved along

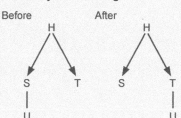

Before    After

T would pay cash (or assets) to S. Consideration cannot be in shares as T may become a subsidiary or associate of S and retain an interest in U. This type of reorganisation may be done if the group wishes to sell S, but retain U.

### Accounting entries:

| | |
|---|---|
| In T's books | Dr Investment in U |
| | Cr Cash |
| In S's books | Dr Cash |
| | Cr Investment in U |

## Reverse acquisitions

Definition

A reverse acquisition occurs when an entity obtains ownership of the shares of another entity, which in turn issues sufficient shares so that the acquired entity has control of the combined entity.

Reverse acquisitions are a method of allowing unlisted companies to obtain a stock exchange quotation by taking over a smaller listed company.

A private entity may arrange to be acquired by a listed entity. The public entity issues shares to the private entity so that the private entity's shareholders end up controlling the listed entity. Legally, the public entity is the parent, but the substance of the transaction is that the private entity has acquired the listed entity.

**Exam focus**

Group reorganisations are not examined regularly.

Examination questions include:

- December 2011 – Decany

# Group statement of cash flows

In this chapter

- Overview.
- Format of the statement of cash flows.
- Dividends from associates.
- Dividends paid to non-controlling interests.
- Acquisitions and disposals.

## Overview

- A statement of cash flows enables users of the financial statements to assess the **liquidity**, **solvency** and **financial adaptability** of a business.

- **Cash consists of** cash in hand and deposits repayable upon demand less overdrafts. This includes cash held in a foreign currency.

- **Cash equivalents** are '**short term, highly liquid investments that are readily convertible to known amounts of cash and are subject to an insignificant risk of changes in value**' (IAS 7, para 6).

- **Cash flows** are '**inflows and outflows of cash and cash equivalents**' (IAS 7, para 6).

## Format of the statement of cash flows

**IAS 7 Statement of cash flows** requires that the statement is split into three section – operating, investing and financing.

**DEF Group statement of cash flows for the year ended 31 December 20X6**

| | $000 | $000 |
|---|---|---|
| **Cash flows from operating activities** | | |
| Profit before tax | X | |
| Adjustments for: | | |
| Depreciation charge | X | |
| Impairment of goodwill | X | |
| Profit on sale of non-current assets | (X) | |
| Investment income | (X) | |
| Finance costs | X | |
| Operating profit before working capital changes | X | |
| Increase in inventories | (X) | |
| Increase in receivables | (X) | |
| Increase in payables | X | |
| Cash generated from operations | | X |
| Interest paid | (X) | |
| Income tax paid | (X) | |
| **Net cash inflow from operating activities** | | X |
| **Cash flows from investing activities** | | |
| Dividends received from associate | X | |
| Interest received | X | |
| Purchase of property, plant and equipment | (X) | |
| Proceeds from sale of property | X | |
| Acquisition of subsidiary, net of cash acquired | (X) | |
| Net cash used in investing activities | | (X) |

### Cash flows from financing activities

| | | |
|---|---|---|
| Issue of ordinary share capital | X | |
| Repayment of loan | (X) | |
| Dividends paid to NCI | (X) | |
| Dividends paid to parent shareholders | (X) | |
| | ——— | |
| Net cash used in financing activities | | (X) |
| | | ——— |

### Net increase in cash and cash equivalents

| | |
|---|---|
| | X |
| Cash and cash equivalents brought forward | X |
| Cash and cash equivalents carried forward | ——— |
| | X |
| | ——— |

## Dividends from associates

To find the dividend reconcile the opening and closing balance of the investment in the associate.

| | $000 |
|---|---|
| Associate b/fwd | X |
| Share of profit of associate | X |
| Cash dividend received (**bal fig**) | (X) |
| | ——— |
| Associate c/fwd | X |
| | ——— |

## Dividends paid to non-controlling interests

Reconcile the opening to closing balance and the cash dividend paid is the balancing figure.

|  | $000 |
|---|---|
| NCI b/fwd | X |
| Add: NCI on sub acquisition | X |
| Add: NCI share of profit | X |
| Less: NCI on sub disposal | (X) |
| Cash dividend paid (bal. fig) | (X) |
| NCI c/fwd | X |

## Acquisitions and disposals

The figure shown is the net figure of two items.

*   The cash spent on the purchase or received on the sale of the subsidiary.

*   The cash balances (or overdraft). acquired or disposed of with a subsidiary.

These two figures can be picked up very quickly from the question paper.

The impact of subsidiary acquisitions and disposals will need to be factored into your workings throughout.

Exam focus

Recent examination questions include:

- March/June 2016 – Weston
- December 2013 – Angel

# 25

## UK GAAP

**In this chapter**

- UK GAAP.
- FRS 102.
- Companies Act.

## P2 UK

Exam Focus

This chapter is relevant for those who are taking the P2 UK paper.

## UK GAAP

Guidance about the accounting standards that UK companies should apply is found within FRS 100 Application of Financial Reporting Requirements. The rules are as follows:

- Listed groups must prepare their accounts under IFRS.

  - However, the companies within the group can take advantage of disclosure exemptions outlined in FRS 101 when preparing their individual (non-consolidated) financial statements.

- Other UK companies will apply FRS 102 The Financial Reporting Standard Applicable in the UK and the Republic Ireland unless:

  - they voluntarily choose to apply IFRS, or

  - they are a micro entity and choose apply FRS 105 The Financial Reporting Standard Applicable to th Micro Entities Regime.

# FRS 102

FRS 102 is a single standard that is organised by topic. Although FRS 102 is based on the IFRS for SMEs Standard, there are differences. Some of these differences are examinable in the UK P2 syllabus.

## Financial statement presentation

- To comply with Companies Act, FRS 102 allows a 'true and fair over-ride'. If compliance with FRS 102 is inconsistent with the requirement to give a true and fair view, the directors must depart from FRS 102 to the extent necessary to give a true and fair view. Particulars of any such departure, the reasons for it and its effect are disclosed.

## Statement of cash flows

- Under FRS 102, small entities, mutual life assurance companies, pension funds and certain investment funds are not required to produce a statement of cash flows. This exemption does not exist under the IFRS for SMEs Standard.

## Consolidated and separate financial statements

- Under the IFRS for SMEs Standard, a parent need not present consolidated financial statements if the parent is itself a subsidiary, and its ultimate parent (or any intermediate parent) produces consolidated general purpose financial statements.

- FRS 102 amends the above to comply with Companies Act. In particular, consolidated financial statements do not need to be produced if the parent, and group headed by it, qualify as small.

## Investments in associates

- FRS 102 explicitly clarifies that an investment in an associate cannot be equity accounted in the individual financial statements of a company that is a parent. Instead, the investment in associate can be held at cost of fair value.

- Under FRS 102, the cost of an associate should include transaction costs. These are excluded from the cost of the associate under the IFRS for SMEs Standard.

### Investments in joint ventures

- FRS 102 explicitly clarifies that an investment in a jointly controlled entity cannot be equity accounted in the individual financial statements of a company that is a parent. Instead it can be held at cost of fair value.

### Intangible assets

- Under FRS 102, an intangible asset arising from development activity can be recognised if certain criteria are met. These criteria are broadly the same as under IAS 38. According to the IFRS for SMEs Standard, research

and development expenditure is always written off to profit or loss.

- Under FRS 102, intangible assets can be held under the cost model or the revaluation model. The IFRS for SMEs Standard does not permit the revaluation model.

### Business combinations and goodwill

- According to FRS 102, Negative goodwill is recognised on the statement of financial position immediately below goodwill. It should be followed by a subtotal of the net amount of goodwill and the negative goodwill. Under the IFRS for SMEs Standard, negative goodwill is recognised immediately in profit or loss.

### Government grants

- Under FRS 102, two methods of recognising government grants are allowed:

- The performance model
- The accruals model
- Under the IFRS for SMEs Standard, only the performance model is permitted.

## Borrowing costs

- Under FRS 102, an entity may capitalise borrowing costs that are directly attributable to the construction, acquisition or production of a qualifying asset. Under the IFRS for SMEs Standard, all borrowing costs are recognised as an expense in profit or loss.

## Employee Benefits

- Under FRS 102, the projected unit credit method must be used to estimate the defined benefit obligation. In contrast, the IFRS for SMEs Standard permits some simplified estimation techniques.

## Related parties

- FRS 102 permits an additional exemption from the disclosure of related party transactions. FRS 102 states that disclosures need not be given of transactions entered into between two or more members of a group, provided that any subsidiary which is a party to the transaction is wholly owned by such a member.

## Income tax

- FRS 102 adopts a profit or loss approach to the recognition of deferred tax. In contrast, the IFRS for SMEs Standard conceptualises deferred tax through the statement of financial position.

- FRS 102 uses the concept of permanent differences. The IFRS for SMEs Standard does not use the terminology 'permanent difference'. Instead, it says that deferred tax assets and liabilities are recognised for 'temporary differences'.

## Companies Act

### Single entity financial statements

A company is exempt from the requirement to prepare individual accounts for a financial year if:

- it is itself a subsidiary undertaking
- it has been dormant throughout the whole of that year, and
- its parent undertaking is established under the law of an EEA State.

### Group financial statements

A company subject to the small companies' regime may prepare group accounts for the year.

If not subject to the small companies' regime, a parent company must prepare group accounts for the year unless one of the following applies:

- A company is exempt from the requirement to prepare group accounts it is itself a wholly owned subsidiary of parent undertaking.
- A parent company is exempt from the requirement to prepare group accounts if, under section 405 of Companies Act all of its subsidiary undertakings could excluded from consolidation.

A subsidiary undertaking may be excluded from consolidation where:

- severe longterm restrictions substantia hinder the exercise of the rights of the parent company over the assets or management of that undertaking
- the information necessary for the preparation of group accounts cannot be obtained without disproportionate expense or undue delay
- the interest of the parent company is held exclusively with a view to subsequent resale.

It is important to review the most recent P2 UK papers to see the types of UK-specific questions that are asked.

# References

The Board (2016) *Conceptual Framework for Financial Reporting*. London: IFRS Foundation.

The Board (2016) *IAS 1 Presentation of Financial Statements*. London: IFRS Foundation.

The Board (2016) *IAS 2 Inventories*. London: IFRS Foundation.

The Board (2016) *IAS 7 Statement of Cash Flows*. London: IFRS Foundation.

The Board (2016) *IAS 8 Accounting Policies, Changes in Accounting Estimates and Errors*. London: IFRS Foundation.

The Board (2016) *IAS 10 Events after the Reporting Period*. London: IFRS Foundation.

The Board (2016) *IAS 12 Income Taxes*. London: IFRS Foundation.

The Board (2016) *IAS 16 Property, Plant and Equipment*. London: IFRS Foundation.

The Board (2016) *IAS 19 Employee Benef* London: IFRS Foundation.

The Board (2016) *IAS 20 Accounting for Government Grants and Disclosure of Government Assistance*. London: IFRS Foundation.

The Board (2016) *IAS 21 The Effects of Changes in Foreign Exchange Rates*. London: IFRS Foundation.

The Board (2016) *IAS 23 Borrowing Costs*. London: IFRS Foundation.

The Board (2016) *IAS 24 Related Party Disclosures*. London: IFRS Foundation.

The Board (2016) *IAS 27 Separate Financ* *Statements*. London: IFRS Foundation.

The Board (2016) *IAS 28 Investments in Associates and Joint Ventures*. London: IFRS Foundation.

The Board (2016) *IAS 32 Financial Instruments: Presentation*. London: IFRS Foundation.

The Board (2016) *IAS 33 Earnings per Share*. London: IFRS Foundation.

The Board (2016) *IAS 34 Interim Financial Reporting*. London: IFRS Foundation.

The Board (2016) *IAS 36 Impairment of Assets*. London: IFRS Foundation.

The Board (2016) *IAS 37 Provisions, Contingent Liabilities and Contingent Assets*. London: IFRS Foundation.

The Board (2016) *IAS 38 Intangible Assets*. London: IFRS Foundation.

The Board (2016) *IAS 40 Investment Property*. London: IFRS Foundation.

The Board (2016) *IAS 41 Agriculture*. London: IFRS Foundation.

The Board (2016) *IFRS 1 First-time Adoption of International Financial Reporting Standards*. London: IFRS Foundation.

The Board (2016) *IFRS 2 Share-based Payment*. London: IFRS Foundation.

The Board (2016) *IFRS 3 Business Combinations*. London: IFRS Foundation.

The Board (2016) *IFRS 5 Non-current Assets Held for Sale and Discontinued Operations*. London: IFRS Foundation.

The Board (2016) *IFRS 7 Financial Instruments: Disclosure*. London: IFRS Foundation.

The Board (2016) *IFRS 8 Operating Segments*. London: IFRS Foundation.

The Board (2016) *IFRS 9 Financial Instruments*. London: IFRS Foundation.

The Board (2016) *IFRS 10 Consolidated Financial Statements*. London: IFRS Foundation.

The Board (2016) *IFRS 11 Joint Arrangements*. London: IFRS Foundation.

The Board (2016) *IFRS 12 Disclosure of Interests in Other Entities*. London: IFRS Foundation.

The Board (2016) *IFRS 13 Fair Value Measurement.* London: IFRS Foundation.

The Board (2016) *IFRS 15 Revenue from Contracts with Customers.* London: IFRS Foundation.

The Board (2016) *IFRS 16 Leases.* London: IFRS Foundation.

The Board (2016) *IFRS Practice Statement: Management Commentary.* London: IFRS Foundation.

The Board (2015) *IFRS for SMEs Standard.* London: IFRS Foundation.

# Index

# R

# S

# U